Name _____

Alphabetical order

a b c d e f g h i j k l m n o p q r s t u v w x y z

A Put these animals into alphabetical order.
The first one has been done for you.

fox   seal   bear   penguin

bear   _____   _____   _____

B Do the same with these words.

kangaroo   otter   daffodil   rose   Sue   Nicholas
bear   fox   bluebell   tulip   Alison   Zoe

C Do the same with these.

gloves   boots
tie   hat
dress   scarf

Alphabetical order   1

Plurals

We say one fox . . .   but two foxes.

Add -es to these words.

   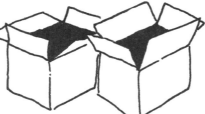      

one box   two _____   one glass   two _____

one dress   three _____   one bus   two _____

one match   four _____   one switch   two _____

Opposites

A Write the opposites of these words.

hot _____   wet _____

fast _____   night _____

We can make opposites by putting **un-** in front of some words.

happy   un + happy = unhappy

B Add un- to these words.

well _____   safe _____

pack _____   tie _____

load _____   do _____

lock _____   lucky _____

Word families

A The heat family

These words all belong to the h**eat** family because they all have the **eat** sound in them. Can you find them in the word search?

eat   heat
cheat   beat
seat   meat
treat

c	h	e	a	t	h
b	d	r	t	r	e
e	a	t	r	e	a
a	t	s	e	a	t
t	m	e	a	t	m

B Sort these words into their families.

lot	not	bet	old	vet	bold	cot	set
fold	hold	met	pot	sold	get	got	

hot

cold

wet

Word families: -eat, -ot, -old, -et

Word families

A Sort these words into the **ea** family and the **ee** family.

| meal | cheese | beans | see | sea | week |
| weak | cheek | meat | sheet | | |

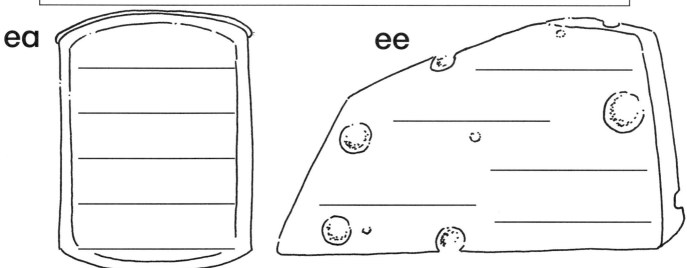

ea

ee

Think of two more **ea** and **ee** words. Write them here.

_____ _____

B Complete these sentences using **week** or **weak**.

1. He was too _____ to get out of bed.

2. He was ill for a _____.

C Complete these sentences using **see** or **sea**.

1. The _____ was very rough.

2. Can you _____ that boat?

Word families/homophones

What am I?

  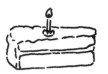

orange   butter   egg   birthday cake   ice lolly   carrot

I am sweet.
I am made of ice.
I have a stick.

I am an _____.

I grow on a tree.
I am a fruit.
My name is a colour.

I am an _____.

I am hard on the outside.
I am soft on the inside.
You can eat me boiled, fried or scrambled.

I am an _____.

I grow in the ground.
I am a vegetable.
I am orange in colour.

I am a _____.

I am yellow.
I am soft.
People spread me on bread.

I am _____.

I am sweet.
People cut me in slices.
I often have candles on top of me.

I am a _____.

Riddles

Choose the right word

1. We put _____ on bread. (butter/batter)

2. We _____ bread in the oven. (eat/bake)

3. John eats bread with his _____. (soap/soup)

4. Hayley ate _____ for dinner. (fish/dish)

5. We cut bread with a _____. (knife/fork)

6. If you don't get it right _____ again. (dry/try)

7. He fell _____ the stairs. (up/down)

8. He was in a hurry so he _____ to the shops. (walked/ran)

9. The sun shone and the sea was _____. (blue/blew)

10. I am going to London next _____. (week/weak)

Word choice

Adding -ing

Look at these words.

hide   **hiding**

When a word ends in an **e**, we drop the **e** before adding **ing**.

A Add **ing** to these words. Remember to drop the **e** first!

ride + ing = _____   give + ing = _____

dive + ing = _____   bake + ing = _____

wake + ing = _____   shake + ing = _____

write + ing = _____   share + ing = _____

 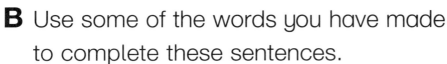

B Use some of the words you have made to complete these sentences.

1. He is _____ some bread.

2. She is _____ a letter.

3. They are _____ into the water.

4. He is _____ a horse.

5. The men are _____ hands.

Describing

| dark | old | hot | fast | secret |
| loud | broken | empty | full | |

 a _____ den

 a _____ chair

 an _____ man

 a _____ car

 a _____ bottle

 an _____ bottle

 a _____ day

 a _____ night

 a _____ noise

What are they saying?

Write what you think they are saying.

Writing dialogue (speech bubbles)

Using 'and'

Look at these sentences:

Mars has red rocks.

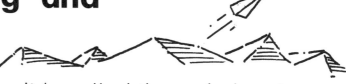
It is called the red planet.

We can join these two sentences with **and** to make one longer sentence:

Mars has red rocks **and** is called the red planet.

A Match each beginning to its ending
The first one has been done for you.

A door opened in the space ship   and lay in the sun.
                                 and fly to Mars.
She came out of the sea   and is made of fire.
She wants to be an astronaut   and a funny green man came out.
It was a clear night
The sun is very hot   and the stars were bright.

B Join these sentence with the word **and**.
The first one has been done for you.

1. She opened the box.   She took out a ring.

   <u>She opened the box and took out the ring.</u>

2. The van stopped.   A man got out.

   _____

3. He read the book.   He took it back to the library.

Adding -ing

Look at these words.

sit   **sitting**

Some words double the last letter before adding **ing**.

A Add **ing** to these words. Remember to double the last letter first!

sit + ing = _____   run + ing = _____

swim + ing = _____   win + ing = _____

wet + ing = _____   put + ing = _____

shut + ing = _____   hum + ing = _____

B Use some of the words you have made to complete these sentences.

1. He is _____ away from the flying saucer.

2. He is _____ on the chair.

3. She is _____ in the sea.

4. Jo is _____ the race.

5. He is _____ the door.

6. They are _____ the toys away.

Elephants

A Look for these words in the word search.

happy   old   young   thin   tall   fat
smile   patchwork   joke

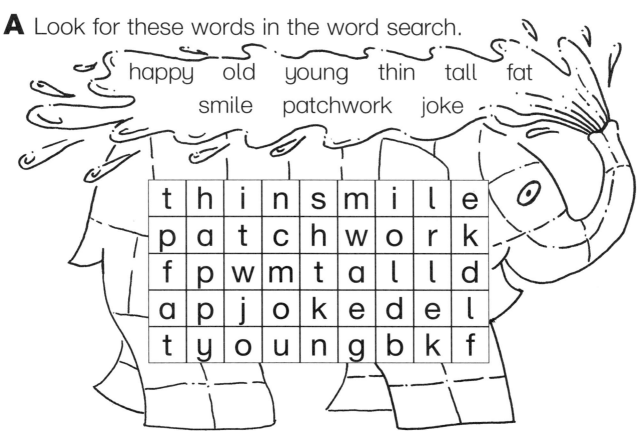

t	h	i	n	s	m	i	l	e
p	a	t	c	h	w	o	r	k
f	p	w	m	t	a	l	l	d
a	p	j	o	k	e	d	e	l
t	y	o	u	n	g	b	k	f

B Choose a good word from the word search to write under each of these elephants.

  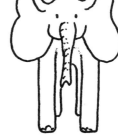

_____   _____   _____   _____

_____   _____   _____

Word search/adjectives

Alliterative animals

A Read the caption and colour the pictures.

A brown bear

A pink pig

An orange orang-utan

B Choose a word that begins with the same letter as the name of the animal. The first one has been done for you.

| lazy   happy   odd   clever   ~~wiggly~~   busy |

a _wiggly_ worm

a _____ lion

a _____ hedgehog

a _____ cat

an _____ octopus

a _____ bee

Alliteration/adjectives

Animal homes

These animals are lost. Can you help them find their way home?

Which animal lives underground? _____

Which one carries its home wherever it goes? _____

Which one uses its home to catch insects? _____

Monster goes to school

Draw how you think the story will end. Then write about it

Writing a story: predicting an ending

Sentences

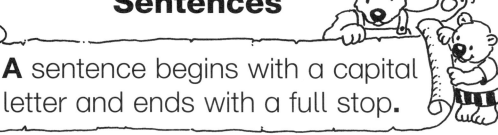

A sentence begins with a capital letter and ends with a full stop.

A Copy these sentences. Begin each one with a capital letter. Put a full stop at the end.

1. once upon a time there were three bears

   _____

2. the ugly sisters went to the ball

   _____

3. the shoemaker cut out the shoes at night

   _____

B The words in these sentences are mixed up.
Write each sentence correctly.
Don't forget the capital letters and full stops!

1. words mixed these are up

   _____

2. sentence with begins a letter capital a

   _____

3. sentence stop ends full a with a

   _____

Sentences: capital letters and full stops/word order

Plurals (more than one)

When a word ends in **-y** we make it plural (more than one) by **dropping the y** and **adding -ies**:

one diar**y**, but two diar**ies**; one fair**y**, but two fair**ies**.

A Find the plurals of these words in the word search. Write them in the list.

b	e	r	r	i	e	s	m	d
f	a	m	i	l	i	e	s	a
l	c	r	i	g	s	r	t	i
i	l	d	l	a	d	i	e	s
e	d	b	a	b	i	e	s	i
s	p	a	r	t	i	e	s	e
c	o	u	n	t	r	i	e	s

berry _____

family _____

party _____

fly _____

daisy _____   country _____

lady _____   baby _____

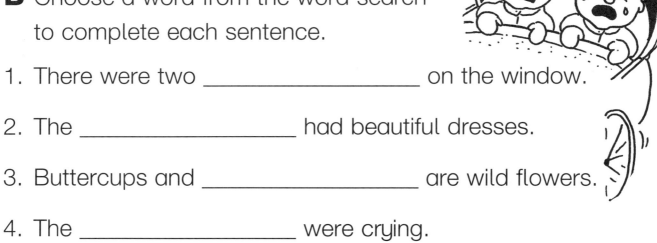

B Choose a word from the word search to complete each sentence.

1. There were two _____ on the window.

2. The _____ had beautiful dresses.

3. Buttercups and _____ are wild flowers.

4. The _____ were crying.

Plurals   18

Using 'and' or 'but'

Look at these sentences:

The new duckling was ugly **and** his mother was sad.

The duckling was ugly **but** it grew into a beautiful swan.

A Match each beginning to its ending. The first one has been done for you.

Cinderella wanted to go to the ball — but her sisters wouldn't let her.
She tried on a glass slipper
Jack planted the magic beans
Sleeping Beauty pricked her finger

and slept for a hundred years.
and a beautiful beanstalk grew.
and it fitted.

B Join these sentences with **and** or **but**.

1. Thumbelina climbed on the swallow's wing _____ they flew away.

2. An old man asked him for a cake _____ he said no.

3. He was called the Happy Prince _____ he was always crying.

4. Jack cut down the beanstalk _____ the giant was killed.

Rhymes

If the word rhymes with **wed** colour the shape **blue**.
If the word rhymes with **pen** colour the shape **yellow**.

If the word rhymes with **bee** colour the shape **brown**.

If the word rhymes with **cry** colour the shape **red**.
If the word rhymes with **dad** colour the shape **green**.

If the word rhymes with **old** colour the shape **orange**.

Words on the butterfly: mad, told, shed, lad, dry, pad, hen, try, led, see, free, sad, had, my, fed, bold, den, bad, fly, bed

Rhymes

is and are

We say:

The **caterpillar is** hungry.   The **caterpillars are** hungry.

Complete these sentences using **is** or **are**.

1. The sun _____ hot.
2. The sea _____ cold.
3. They _____ swimming.
4. The market _____ busy.
5. The people _____ shopping.
6. The birds _____ singing.

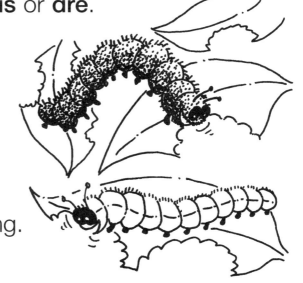

was and were

We say:

He was hungry.   **They were** hungry.

Complete these sentences using **was** or **were**.

1. The ice lolly _____ melting.
2. They _____ digging up the road.
3. Mr. Johnson _____ very happy.
4. The books _____ very interesting.
5. The gates _____ closed at six o'clock.
6. The cat _____ sleeping under the tree.

Vowels

The vowels are the letters **a**, **e**, **i**, **o** and **u**.

A Find the vowels and colour them in.

B Find the words that begin with a vowel. Write them here.

insect   caterpillar   bee   _____

elephant   worm   shell   _____

underground   ant   fly   _____

open   closed   wing   _____

wasp   centipede   legs   _____

C Complete these names by adding a vowel.

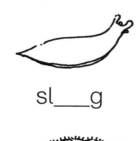   

sl__g   l__dybird   m__th

caterp__llar   be__   sn__il

Adventure World

Write a sentence for each of these rides. Make them sound exciting! The first one has been done for you.

Roller Coaster

fast   exciting   up   down   speed   breath-taking

Ride our roller coaster at breath-taking speed.

Log Splash

exciting   water   wet   spray   shower

Starship

travel   stars   amazing   worlds   speed of light

Adventure Trail

explore   rocks   woods   lake   waterfall   rope bridge

Writing: advertising slogans/descriptive sentences

Questions and answers

This is a question mark.

It is put at the end of a question instead of a full stop.

A Put a question mark at the end of these questions.
Then write the answers.

1. What is your name

    _____

2. How old are you

    _____

3. Where do you live

    _____

    _____

4. What is your favourite colour

    _____

    _____

5. What is your favourite food

    _____

6. What is your favourite story

    _____

B Write a question for a friend to answer.

Don't forget the question mark.

Question marks/writing questions and answers